A Beginner's Guide To Periscope
By Dave Brett

Content Page

Content Page

Introduction to Periscope

Periscope - yet another social media bandwagon to jump on!

Sometimes, I don't know how I cope keeping up all the social media platforms out there? So, will this platform be the new best thing or a flop?

My verdict on Periscope? In a nutshell, it's fun, easy to use, gains crazy engagement and makes it so simple to share in the moment. Simply put, you would be silly not to start Periscoping.

I'm having loads of fun with this new social media platform. Periscope is slowly becoming my new addiction and I'm constantly bumping into others who feel the same way as I do about the new live-streaming app.

In this book, I wanted to share with you my personal journey of how I got started with Periscope and help you to build up the courage to give it a go and follow in my pursuit.

Periscope would not have been possible in the past, but smartphone technology and data connectivity is on the rise and now is the time for live streaming. It's time to look into the possibilities of live broadcasting through the Periscope platform.

Periscope is easy to set up and get started

Periscope is very simple to use:

- Download the app.
- Sign up for a Periscope account.
- Turn on the Twitter and Location ticker.
- Enter a title and click "broadcast".
- Once you're live, you just put together a "Scope" on the fly and click to stop broadcasting once you've finished.

Job done! No editing or uploading required. It's so easy compared to traditional video sharing methods.

Those who follow you can keep streaming along until you're finished.

When I normally think of capturing my day on video and sharing events in the moment with my audience on social media, the pure effort and pain of editing and uploading soon puts me off.

Hasn't everyone been saying that video is the next big thing for the web? I think it's finally happening with Periscope.

Video is difficult and time-consuming to put together. In fact, I have 47GB of video footage sitting on my hard drive with no plans for it to ever see the light of day. Isn't that depressing? I'm sure many of you can relate. However, with Periscope kicking off, I have a feeling that this will soon be a thing of the past.

Instantly Live with your audience

Periscope simply delivers live footage that your audience want to see and puts it all together so easily.

Most importantly, Periscope is fun!

Everyday many users are finding fun ways to use Periscope, and more are being discovered all the time. This opens up many new opportunities to explore.

Think of podcasting as an example. Scheduling, editing, uploading. It all takes a lot of time to put together. Periscope can be a great platform for hosting interviews and have your audience join in on the conversation and add to the discussion.

Fitness instructors can host daily workouts at set times. Think how awesome it could be to host Yoga lessons? Why not offer a sample session on Periscope to show the audience how good you, then encourage them towards your paid subscription package for more in-depth training.

How about product reviews? Wouldn't it be cool to have your audience in the chat ask the exact questions they want the answers for?

How about travel bloggers? They can share a trip while they are actually on it. There's no need to wait for the video to be edited or the blog to be written, just share the destination live with your audience.

What about lifestyle coaches? Wouldn't it be cool to run a workshop each day and motivate, teach and help people directly on a range of subjects.

How about running a cooking show if you are food blogger? You could run through the step-by-step cooking instructions for a recipe.

Create arts and crafts together, with guided instructions? Read children's books at night time, if you are a book publisher? The possibilities are endless for Periscope, and are their to be explored. If you have a passion and want to share it with your audience, live content is a fantastic way to make it happen.

Periscope: Just do it!

Get the ball rolling and take action, do your first Periscope now!

First Periscope? Don't worry, just keep rolling, your first 50 might be terrible, but just learn by doing it!

What was your first Facebook status? Exactly, who cares, it's just important to start today. Download the app now and get Scoping!

Start your first stream by saying that its your first Periscope session. Just relax, see who joins in and practise a little.

It's important to not complain about the phone that you have or if your signal is terrible, the whole idea is to put all this negativity to one side and get to work Periscoping.

You've got hearts (Periscopes equivalent of "likes") flowing, your WiFi or 3G connection is cutting out, your battery's going flat! I know, I've been there. In fact, all Periscopers have been there, but just keep going and keep on getting better and better, each and every time.

The most important step towards becoming a Periscoper is to just start doing it. Trial and error is key, give several different ideas a go. Keep working at it and see what gets a great response from your audience.

At the moment Periscope is fairly new, but it is incredibly engaging. Users want to watch interesting scopes by interesting people.

The audience will ask you loads of great questions. My advice is to just follow their lead, see what they want to get out of your stream and experiment with what you can create.

Follow those already on Periscope

Periscope is new, so surround yourself with others who are also Periscoping regularly to see how they do it. Remember to give them plenty of hearts and engage with comments.

This is the best way to be a part of the Periscope community. Jump into each others scopes and surround yourself with other scopers. Learn, scope, discover - it's truly the best way to embrace Periscope.

Here are some of my favourites Scopers to get you started:

- ATravelingToad
- Nomad is beautiful
- Kerwin McKenzie
- Johnnyjet
- Travel with kat
- the crowded planet
- live dream discover
- Opptravelers
- TravelDaveuk

It's good to observe how they scope, how they share their experiences and how they answer questions from their audience and engage with new members.

Being a part of the Periscope Community is the best way to learn as a new Periscoper.

Engage and answer your audience's questions

Think of every Periscope like a podcast interview, but with changing and more interesting scenery, and without having to edit afterwards. You can just click broadcast, get the ball rolling and you're away with your Q&A.

It's important to answer questions from your audience to keep the narrative alive. Ask what people are generally thinking and they will feel a sense of belonging when you take the time to respond.
Of course, it's impossible to answer all of them, but make an effort and more questions will come your way.

You can also ask your audience questions:

* Where are you from?
* Anyone travelled here before?
* Do you have any travel questions I can answer?

This can spark a conversation and open up your audience to ask questions. If you feel brave you can ask them what you should do next. I've found this really entertaining at times, such as being asked to wave at locals, buy some street food from a local vendor, turn down a road, go into a shop and look around a park.

This is part of the fun of live broadcasting, you never know what might happen. Have fun with it, and entertain and engage with your audience.

Hearts on Periscope are important

Hearts indicate to Periscope how popular your current Scope is while its live. The more hearts, the more chance you have of new viewers joining your Periscope Chat.

It's also indicates to viewers whether they should follow you or not, as a large number of hearts means you're probably doing something worth seeing. The bottom line is that hearts are important!

This is why it's smart to surround yourself with other first-time Periscopers and offer to heart each others Scopes. You can jump in to watch and measure each others progress and heart each other. This is a really useful, collaborative and fun way of boosting your engagement.

You can also ask your audience to send hearts, such as for the people you happen to be filming - just ask your audience to send some hearts as a way of saying hello.

It's also nice to mention the Periscope account of anybody you're filming to cross promote and help the audience with names in the comment section as they may wish to ask them questions directly or follow them on Periscope as well.

It's hard to get the hearts flowing at first, but by reminding and encouraging viewers to start sending them, you'll quickly get going. Basically, the more hearts you get, the more you will start to notice an increase in traffic flow. Viewers normally don't mind giving hearts, but they often forget to do so. Get the ball rolling by asking nicely and you will notice a spike in hearts.

It's also just as important to thank viewers for giving hearts as this then encourages even more.

In a nutshell, hearts are good. We all love hearts on Periscope, so keep the hearts going. OK, enough about hearts, you get the picture, enjoy!

Start your scope with a scenic view

Isn't it awesome to share *your* world with *the* world.

It normally takes some time to jump into a scope, you won't instantly have everyone tuning in. It will take some time to build a following.

It's nice to start off with some sort of view to build up the audience before you start talking, around 10 seconds will do it, this will ensure that you will have a few people in listening to your conversation rather than everyone joining mid-conversation.

Periscope also captures your first shot as the title screenshot for that Periscope, so you want it to look pretty rather than a shot of the ground or your feet, who wants to see that?

It's a good idea not to dive straight into the subject matter your title suggests. At the start of your scope, just open up the group instead, welcome people as they come in, and get the party started before giving out the golden nuggets.

The perfect length of a scope.

To be honest, this doesn't really matter, it all depends on how good you are at telling a story and keeping momentum within your scope.

Showing where you are, communicating to your audience and keeping the party going plays an important role in keeping your scope in full flow.

Keep an eye on numbers joining, so you can spot any decline in interest, or people dropping out.

Every time you scope, think back to what caused that decline. What did you do, or not do, to lose the interest of your viewers?

Use knowledge gained from each Scope to go forward with what worked and drop what didn't.

As you can tell there is no right or wrong answer for length of time, if you have an engaged audience with your scope, keep it rocking until you feel a need to stop.

Consistency is king

Find interesting subjects to film each and every day on Periscope. Things you might not expect to be interesting could be a hit on Periscope. Just try things out!

It's important to do a daily Periscope broadcast for this reason and this reason alone - if new members find your Periscope.TV account, only videos from the past 24 hours appear.

If you have no recent streams, then your Periscope.tv page will be empty. Everybody knows that having an empty shop with empty shelves doesn't look good!

Try to schedule a daily show when starting out to ensure that something is always on your Periscope.TV page, otherwise new viewers to your Periscope will not be impressed when they come to visit.

Daily shows will help to grow an audience with Periscope, make a theme out of it.

Geotagging your scopes is vital to success

Always pin your Periscope geolocation.
If you're travelling, it's very important that you include your geolocation pin.

You do have the option to hide your location, many users do this for privacy reasons as they don't wish to share their home location with others.

However, this feature can work to your advantage. Periscope is rather new and not every country is using Periscope as actively as others, so by sharing your geolocation on Periscope a unique pin will be placed on the Periscope globe that shares out broadcasts from around the world.

Many Periscope users actively use the global feature to locate new broadcasts to follow and wish to explore more exotic locations.

If you're in a unique location that possibly might have not yet been Scoped and can bring a massive audience to your broadcast.

On my recent Trip to the demilitarised zone between North Korea and South Korea, my stream managed to fetch over 500 viewers, and it was just in a car park! It just goes to show that if you can Periscope from a unique location, many people will be interested to see what you're up to.

Battery power limitations with Periscope.

Did you know that one minute of periscoping will drain 1% of your smart phone battery? Yep! This pretty much sucks if you want to do multiple broadcasts throughout the day.

Fear not! The solution to this problem is to carry an external battery pack to charge your device on the go.

I like to use the Anker PowerCore 15600, which will charge your iPhone 6 up to 5 times with a single charge. It also contains a smart chip that acts as a surge to ensure your device powers up and turns off when the charge is complete. It comes with a good warranty too, and is compact enough to tuck away inside a backpack.

Sign up to Periscope Facebook groups

If you want to get into Periscope best to surround yourself with others doing the same.

Facebook is a good way to find groups related to your brand or business.

Periscope is growing in popularity and more Facebook groups are popping up all the time.

As an example, I'm a part of the "Periscope Travel Group" and it's a great place to start and find fellow travel related periscopers.

I like this group, as its new and fairly active. I can see it growing in popularity as more Travel Bloggers start to adapt to Periscope. Come on over and join in the fun.

Find a Periscope Facebook group by searching in the Facebook Search Tab.

ChatterBox for Periscope

One feature of Periscope you have to grasp is that once the content has gone out, it will disappear. This is also the case for any chat messages, so it's not possible to go back and read messages on posted on old Periscope sessions.

ChatterBox is a Chrome extension that aims to solve this.

ChatterBox is an app that lets you go back to read old chat messages through the Google Chrome web browser.

If you missed the messages during a scope, say you were too busy focusing on your cooking class, this allows you to go back and answer viewer questions at a later time.

It's also a great way to run polls with your audience as you can ask dual questions, get viewers to message one another answers and run a live survey, how exciting!

You will need to be running Chrome at the same time as your Periscope, but its easily done if you have a laptop close by.

Sound quality for Periscope

You can make use of your mobile phone's inbuilt microphone, but is this the best solution?

My aim is to encourage you to just get started and create Scopes, but I've heard from talking to others that they are to worried about starting to Periscope due to sound quality. At this stage, this is just being too paranoid. I wouldn't focus too much on the sound quality if its going to stop you from putting together your first 50 scopes, as you should get plenty of practice and a decent audience before you even consider upping sound quality.

in the meantime you could make use of headphones with a built in microphone for sound recording. This will achieve a more up-close recording as they tend to pick up less background noise.

However if you are looking to take your Periscope sessions to the next level you should invest and purchase a Røde SmartLav+, which plugs into any smartphone and instantly starts recording top quality directional sound for your Scopes. It simply clips onto your T-shirt and away you go, awesome top quality sound, its small and compact enough to tuck away in your pocket, too.

Use Katch.me to back up and store your Periscopes

Focus on Periscoping, leave everything else to katch.me

Katch.me does exactly what it says in the name, it captures your Periscope streams and stores them beyond Periscope's 24 hour limit, which is really useful if you wish to re-play or store your Periscopes for the future.

It's both easy and simple to set up. The longer you leave it, the more Periscope streams will be lost, so set it up today and never worry about losing your periscopes ever again.

Katch.me will tweet you a notification when the broadcast has been cached, so you have nothing to worry about and can simply carry on with your travel blogging.

Katch.me has everything covered. Once a month you can schedule a bulk download session, then upload them directly to YouTube (more about this later).

Katch.me has also just announced an auto Facebook upload attachment to Katch.me accounts, this makes publishing your broadcasts to your Facebook page even more simple. Isn't automation great!

Start your Periscope with a creative title.

"Come join me for a Korean BBQ in Seoul" is an example of a title that worked well for me on Periscope.

Don't be robotic with your Periscope titles, its just pure boring, who wants to follow a robot? Forget keywords and hashtags, focus on engaging your audience.

Your audience will be somewhat selective with which broadcast they want to engage with, especially if you plan on Periscoping each and every day.

Your Periscope title will pop up on your followers' phone screens when you start a broadcast. This is your window of opportunity to bring them into your live stream.

Also, it's good to never forget replayers - the audience that might not catch the live stream, but views your Periscope channel within the 24 hour window. It's always worth giving them a mention by going all "Back to the Future and welcoming replayers during your live stream. It makes everyone feel at home, and is a useful way to gain extra hearts and boost engagement.

Also, note that you are limited to Twitter's 140 characters in the title, so you'll want to avoid going hashtag crazy, even though they can be effective.

Taking all this into account, you have to be creative with your Periscope Titles.

I've noticed that the use of Emojis, when selected well, can work wonders for screen notification engagement. They normally create a pop art effect that draws people into your Periscope from their phone screen.

The shorter the title, the better. If you can write it in a way that sparks curiosity or hints that it will be useful, this can work wonders.

Examples that I've seen recently:

• Look what I've found on the beach in Florida
• Check out this sky view in Bangkok
• I've never seen a storm like this
• Want to join me for some Thai street food
• Need help planning your next adventure
• Lets go on a walk around Singapore
• Who fancies a Tuk Tuk ride

I've just picked these random titles from memory, but they are the ones that stuck with me. All are short, to the point and engaging in their own way and drew me into viewing the Scope.

You don't have to use all the characters just because you have them. It's ok to be selective, but always aim to be inviting. This is not about you, its about sharing what you're doing or seeing with an audience and growing a little mini community around your personal journey.

Easily moderate and block users during your live broadcast

You can easily do your own admin with Periscope. If a viewer in your Periscope room is posting nasty comments or trolling, you can easily block them by tapping on the user name and selecting "block". This avoids a lot of hassle and fuss. It's easy to moderate your own live stream during the broadcast.

Periscope eats mobile data like a German drinks beer at Oktoberfest.

You will have to get used to buying 3G mobile data packages as you move around.

This is one of the key issues with Periscope - if you want to become a good Periscope user, you're going to have to invest in plenty of 3G mobile data.

In some countries, this doesn't come cheap. On my recent visit to South Korea, the cheapest option I could find was roughly £20 for 1GB of 3G data at the 7/11 airport store.

However, in some countries, such as Thailand, I've managed to get a whopping 9GB of data for as little as £12. This makes Thailand an awesome destination to Periscope, they even have 4G connection in some areas, such as in Chiang Mai. It's just hit and miss from country to country.

Try to turn off all auto-updates on your smart phone when travelling and only use 3G data for Periscope.

You can use free WiFi hotspots, but this limits you to Scoping from indoors. What if you want to walk outside?

Yep, your Periscope broadcast will simply cut out. That's why you should aim at reserving your Periscope streams for 3G and use WiFi hotspots for everything else. This will allow you to capture your travels in the moment and remain mobile.

GiffGaff has some affordable UK 3G/4G data bundles for your smartphone. In the UK you can order a free SIM card with GiffGaff to be sent to your hostel/hotel and active a 500MB data package for £5 or a 1GB data package for £7.50. That's by far the cheapest I've found for travellers to the UK.

For global SIM card advice and tips I like to use one of my favourite travel tech blogs - Too Many Adapters. They have a really useful resource page all about global SIM cards, check it out.

Try to film vertical as much as possible

If possible, try to film in vertical mode. The reason for this is that users in your Scope can type messages more easily.

If your scope is broadcast horizontally, it can make it tricky for viewers using phones such as the iPhone 6+, as the phone is just too big to type messages in horizontal mode.

Messages are good to keep the conversation flowing and the audience engaged with your Scope.

Upload your Periscopes straight to YouTube

This step is purely experimental at this point, but I would like to offer my findings from the tests I've been conducting.

Once you've cached your Periscope broadcast with Katch.me, you can easily download it from the Katch website. Katch has their own video format, but this isn't an issue as it's YouTube-compatible.

Create a simple Periscope YouTube cover art on Canva, then upload the Katch file to your YouTube account. Do 10 minutes of SEO research with Long Tail Pro to better optimise your video for search, then hey presto - you have content on your YouTube page!

I'm currently creating a Periscope-specific playlist on my YouTube page, using the same Periscope themed YouTube cover art for each video scope and mentioning that the video was a Periscope broadcast.

Following these simple steps, after one week I've noticed a handful of views and $0.90 of revenue from Google AdSense.

I know that's not a lot, but over time, the more interesting your Periscopes get, the more you'll capture and grow a YouTube audience.

Add brands with the "@" tag and start sponsored Periscope chats.

This can be a smart way to bring in a partnership opportunity through Periscope. Just as brands are happy to sponsor Twitter chats or Podcast episodes, you can pitch Periscope chats as well! They're live, instant, create discussion, are easily moderated and adaptable to plugging a brand by placing a Twitter handle and hashtag in the Scope's title.

Periscope chats can also be scheduled in advance to attract a bigger reach. Have I just let the cat out of the bag again? Sometimes I should stop talking and take action, but there we go. How's that for a tip? Go enjoy and embrace Periscope!

Engage with Twitter through Periscope

This tip is handy when you're starting out with Periscope and already have a decent Twitter following.

As Twitter owns Periscope, they like to work together and cross promote their platforms. Twitter recently dropped stars in favour of hearts to keep the two platforms in line - how lovely!

You can place hashtags in your Periscope title, which will then cross over to your Twitter feed as long as you select Twitter before you press broadcast. This will bring in extra viewers. You can use hashtags such as:

#Travel
#Periscope
#(your destination)
#live
#katch
#tagtribe

This helps create a sort of Netflix viewing for those looking around Twitter for something to view. If your followers happen to stumble across your tweet as they scan through their daily feed, they can jump straight into your broadcast.

Create a tile for your blog and cross-promote

It's easy to create a tile image for your blog to bring awareness to your Periscope channel.

Periscope is rapidly growing, with thousands of new members joining every day. It won't be long until everyone is Periscoping. Create a tile that can easily fit on your blog, then attach it to your Periscope.TV page and share it across all your other social media channels to let your current audience know you're on Periscope. You can easily create and design a tile graphic using simple online graphic design sites such as Canva.

Check out Scope analytics to track your Periscope success

I'm currently using a beta version of fullscope.tv to track and measure my Periscope engagement. It's a little glitchy right now, but the concept works rather well.

You can sign up for free and track the data once you've set up an account. As your Periscopes start to disappear after 24 hours, using fullscope.tv can help keep track of your progress.

It's a smart way to get an overall picture of your progress and compare your scopes over time. This is something that's hard to keep track of manually, as they vanish so quickly. Fullscope.tv solves this, check it out.

Remind them to hit the follow button!

I'm not making this up. Every time you broadcast its not easy to get viewers to follow you back. Don't miss out on growing a nice following who like your broadcasts - all you have to do is explain how they can follow you back.

In the bottom right corner there is a little human-like figure, ask them to hit it to follow you. It's that simple, all you have to do is ask nicely. A large majority of Scopers are unaware of this, so you can easily grab followers by simply pointing this out - simple!

The same goes for asking people to Tweet or share your broadcast with their own communities. Just ask and see what response you get.

Lets get Periscoping!

Thank you for reading my book about getting started with Periscope.

I hope you've enjoyed the read and found it useful.

Remember the most important aspect to getting started is to just do it and learn through practise.

Keep going, follow others, jump into other Scopers broadcasts and grow the community together.

You can also look out for Periscope Summits being held around the world. These can be great places to meet up with other Periscopers.

Please feel free to follow me on Periscope: @Traveldaveuk, I'm excited to share my travels with you. Please feel free to message me your Periscope username and I will happily follow you back and create a list of Periscoping readers in the near future.

Periscope consultancy: One-on-One session.

Thank you for reading my beginners guide to Periscope. If you happen to be a brand or company looking to introduce Periscope into your business and would like some more hands on, one-on-one advice, I currently offer Skype consultations.

This is a one hour session that will offer you unique and innovative ways to set up and operate Periscope for your business.

Email me at dave@traveldave.co.uk if you would like to make use of this service.

I look forward to speaking with you soon and helping your business get started with Periscope.

About the Author

My name is Dave Brett. I'm 25 years old and I was born and raised in Chingford, East London in the United Kingdom.

I have travelled to 85+ countries, studied in Finland, Wales and The Netherlands, and worked and lived in Singapore, Switzerland, Thailand and the USA. This has all been made possible by being frugal and sticking to a backpacker budget. I have no plans to stop any time soon.

I started a travel blog back in 2005 because of an agreement with my mum. Being 15 at the time, travelling solo was out of the question. I had the desire to do it, but my Mum was not happy with me travelling alone around Scandinavia. I agreed to keep my mum up-to-date daily with what I was getting up to if she would let me go.

So, it was either start travel blogging or don't go on the trip at all. I ended up choosing travel blogging and TravelDave.co.uk was born!

From the start, Travel Dave was about my personal journey and travel tales. It wasn't until 2010 when taking a course in Entrepreneurship at Vaasa

University, Finland, that I decided to turn Travel Dave from a way to share my travels with friends and family into a business. I did this by turning Travel Dave into a travel resource for like-minded travellers seeking helpful advice for their own budget backpacking adventures.

Currently, I live a nomadic, location independent lifestyle which allows me to move anywhere around the world and freely go wherever I wish. I'm extremely mobile and never have a permanent location. I sold all my possessions some years ago and travel with a hand luggage-sized backpack that holds everything I own. I spend most of my time backpacking around multiple destinations over a set period of time using travel hacking techniques to save money and extend my travels. Between these big adventures I like to stop travelling for a little while and set up a temporary home for a few months in a new location. All I need to blog is wifi and coffee, which can be found all over the world (very handy). I plan on living this lifestyle until 2019 when I hope to settle down somewhere in Sweden - that's the dream!

Contact The Author

It's great hearing from readers, please feel free to send me an email: dave@traveldave.co.uk

I'm happy to help answer any questions you may have or if you would like to further discuss any points brought up in the book.

I love social media and you can reach out to me in many different ways:
Send me a Tweet, @Traveldaveuk
Post on my Facebook page
Follow my Instagram feed @Traveldaveuk
Pin on my Pinterest
Plus me on: Google+
Watch me on: YouTube
Snapchat: @Davebrettuk
Periscope: @Traveldaveuk

Many different ways to connect!

The best way to keep up-to-date with Travel Dave is to follow my Monthly Newsletter. It's full of useful information about how to travel on a budget as well as following my personal adventure.

Digital Nomad: Work online, Travel the world, live a location independent lifestyle

Are you looking at creating an online business that allows you to live in a location independent lifestyle and travel the world?

Not sure where to start?

Feel free to check out my other book on the Amazon Kindle: <u>Digital Nomad</u>

Anyone can easily create a lifestyle focused towards setting up a business, making money online whilst travelling the world.

This book will help you:

- Kick-start your Business
- Discover Work available online
- How to Work from the road
- Set your Goals
- Build an audience

- The Art of Adapting to the World
- Learn how to invest your first £100 investment
- Research your market
- Finding a Place to Stay
- Organize your productivity

Also explains:

- Creative Generation
- Concept of a Nomad
- What a Digital Nomad is
- Ways to earn money online
- SEO
- Keywords
- Automation
- Passive income
- Creating Schedule's
- Analytics
- Importance of Email List's

Special sections surrounding:

- Creating content to engage an audience
- Chiang Mai, Thailand starter guide
- Basic Gear guide For Digital Nomads
- Setting up a Bank Account
- Setting up a Mobile Phone Abroad
- Pomodoro Technique

- Bullet Journal
- Round the World Flight (RTW)

Issues addressed in this book:

- Morning rituals
- Killing Procrastination
- How to make friends on the road and create a global social circle
- Visa restrictions & Tax for digital Nomads
- How Traditional Employment is Shifting
- How to manage Customer service remotely
- Time to Establish Yourself

Interested to read more? Follow this link to the Amazon Kindle Page: Digital Nomad

Thank you and best of luck with your journey.

Backpacking on a Budget & Travel Advice

I hope you enjoyed reading my book, If you would like to read more about How to travel the World on a Backpackers Budget, I wrote a whole book about this subject called "Travel Hacking".

This book will help you:

• Sell unwanted junk to help supplement your travel funds
• Pack like a pro and explain which gear you should take with you
• Find cheap flights in the most cost effective and time saving way
• Explore affordable travel options such as rail passes
• Buy food on a budget
• Manage your travel budget so you can go longer and further

It also shows you how to:

• Book Round the World flight tickets

- Use air mile schemes to purchase free flights.
- Use Couchsurfing for free accommodation
- Which methods are best for booking Hostels

Special sections concentrating on:

- Alternative sleeping options, such as sleeping in airports
- Looking into travel Insurance options
- How to study abroad
- How to Teach English abroad
- How to arrange Working Holiday Visas for Singapore, Australia, New Zealand, USA and Canada
- Should you travel alone or with a friend
- Keeping on top of health whilst travelling

Issues addressed in this book:

- Choosing travel as a lifestyle choice
- What it takes to be a backpacker - exploring the backpacker mentality
- Travel philosophy and beating conformity
- Using a minimalist approach to travel better

If this sounds awesome, you can buy Travel Hacking for Kindle, just click on this link:

Travel Hacking By Dave Brett

Have a spare minute? I would be extremely grateful for a review

Thank you for reading Periscope A How to guide to Getting started, I hope you found all the information useful and I wish you the best of luck on your new adventure into a location independent lifestyle. It would be great if you could help spread the word about by leaving a review to help other readers discover this book for themselves.

If you enjoyed this book be sure to spread the word, tell a friend who you feel could benefit from this book, or share the book on Facebook or Twitter and help others to discover it.

Thank you for your support in advance, it really means a lot!

Kind regards,
Dave Brett

Disclaimer

Book: Periscope A How to guide to Getting started

Author: David Timothy Brett

Editor: Simon Partridge

dave@traveldave.co.uk

Cover Designer: Tom Van Altena - tominc.nl

(c) Copyright 2015 by David Timothy Brett

Notice of Rights

For information on getting permission for reprints and excerpts, or interested in a discounted bulk purchase of print copies, contact:

dave@traveldave.co.uk

Need an Editor?

Quality of writing is key to a successful eBook, so I use an editor to tidy things up once the content is ready. If you have a great idea for an eBook, but know that your writing isn't perfect, I can highly recommend using a proofreader or editor.

My friend, Simon, provides a professional proofreading and editing service at an affordable price, so I use him for all of my eBooks. He can handle anything, from blog posts and eBooks, to technical writing (he's got a Chemistry PhD for goodness sake).

Email him at **simonpartridge86@gmail.com,** with a few details of the work you need done and he can give you a quote - tell him Travel Dave sent you!

www.ingramcontent.com/pod-product-compliance
Lightning Source LLC
Chambersburg PA
CBHW051223170526
45166CB00005B/2018